T0099179

Trout in the Desert

BWhitehead

Trout in the Desert

On Fly Fishing, Human Habits, and the Cold Waters of the Arid Southwest

Matthew Dickerson

Illustrations by Barbara Whitehead

Heartstreams, Vol. 1

WingsPress

San Antonio, Texas

2015

Trout in the Desert: On Fly Fishing, Human Habits, and the Cold Waters of the Arid Southwest © 2015 by Matthew Dickerson

First Edition

Print Edition ISBN: 978-1-60940-485-7
ePub ISBN: 978-1-60940-486-4
Kindle ISBN: 978-1-60940-487-1
PDF ISBN: 978-1-60940-488-8

Wings Press
627 E. Guenther • San Antonio, Texas 78210
Phone/fax: (210) 271-7805

On-line catalogue and ordering:
www.wingspress.com
All Wings Press titles are distributed to the trade by
Independent Publishers Group • www.ipgbook.com

Library of Congress Cataloging-in-Publication Data:

Dickerson, Matthew T., 1963-
 Trout in the desert : on fly fishing, human habits, and the cold
waters of the arid Southwest / Matthew Dickerson ; Illustrations by
Barbara Whitehead. -- First edition.
    pages cm
 ISBN 978-1-60940-485-7 (cloth / hardcover : alk. paper) -- ISBN
978-1-60940-486-4 (epub ebook) -- ISBN 978-1-60940-487-1
(kindle/mobipocket ebook) -- ISBN (invalid) 978-1-60940-488-8
(library pdf)
 1. Trout fishing--Southwest, New--Anecdotes. 2. Environmental
degradation--Southwest, New. 3. Nature--Effect of human beings
on--Southwest, New. I. Title.
  SH688.U6D53 2015
  639.2'7570979--dc23   2015022510

Contents

The difference between a path and a road is not only the obvious one. A path is little more than a habit that comes with knowledge of a place. It is a sort of ritual familiarity. As a form, it is a form of contact with a known landscape. It is not destructive. It is the perfect adaptation, through experience and familiarity, of movement to place; it obeys the natural contours; such obstacles as it meets it goes around. A road, on the other hand, even the most primitive road, embodies a resistance against the landscape. Its reason is not simply the necessity for movement, but haste. Its wish is to *avoid* contact with the landscape; it seeks so far as possible to go over the country, rather than through it; its aspiration, as we see clearly in the example of our modern freeways, is to be a bridge; its tendency is to translate place into space in order to traverse it with the least effort. It is destructive, seeking to remove or destroy all obstacles in its way.

—Wendell Berry, "A Native Hill"

BWhitehead

Prologue:

Just A Lot of Hot Air

The year I began writing this book, 2013, was also the year I turned fifty, celebrated my twenty-fifth anniversary, began my twenty-fifth year in my current job (teaching at Middlebury College), and saw my oldest son graduate from college and get engaged. These milestones of aging prompted a certain amount of reflection on my career, my family, my past.

I don't enjoy air travel, I don't like being away from my family, and I can't say I like spending all day listening to lectures at conferences. However one of the few benefits of academic travel—and one of the *many* benefits of being a parent and taking long family vacations, driving and camping our way from Vermont to Yellowstone National Park and back—is that by the time I reached my fiftieth birthday I had managed to catch trout on a fly in twenty-five of the United States. New Mexico was the fourth of these, just after Colorado. Texas was the twenty-second, ahead of New Jersey, Oregon and Washington (and, of course, also ahead of all the other twenty-five states in which I had not yet enticed a trout with a fly).

Somewhere between New Mexico and Texas came my first excursion fly-fishing in Arizona. It was early June of 2006. I had a computer science conference in Sedona, and so I flew to Arizona two days early to spend time fishing the Colorado River at Lee's Ferry. Lee's Ferry (which hasn't actually had a working ferry since 1929 when the Navajo Bridge was constructed to span the Colorado River) is now a campground and boat launch in the starkly beautiful Vermillion Cliffs National Monument. It is at the tail end of Glen Canyon, the head of Marble Canyon and the Grand Canyon National Recreation Area, not too far upriver from the confluence of the Little Colorado and the Colorado River—where the Grand Canyon itself is officially said to begin.

I arrived at the Lee's Ferry Lodge at Vermillion Cliffs around midnight after a late drive up from the Phoenix airport. The owner, not wanting to wait up, left the key out in an envelope with my name. I found my room, went to bed, and got up at dawn eager for a day of fishing.

Despite being in the middle of nowhere, the existence of the Lee's Ferry Anglers Fly Shop a hundred yards down from the lodge suggested a fishing culture: at least enough destination anglers (like me) coming during tourist season to support a fly shop and a guide service. As I learned, however, Vermillion Cliffs has a low population at that time of June. (At least it did the year I was there.) The campground up the road at Lee's Ferry would also prove to be nearly empty. The handful of tourists I met at the lodge restaurant over the course of four meals were not in the area to fish, but to watch California condors. Though apparently there were a couple of guided boat trips up into Glen Canyon during the two days I was there, nobody else had come to Lee's Ferry to catch trout. When I went into the fly shop after breakfast to purchase a fishing license and a few local flies—and to get whatever hot local fishing tips they were willing to dispense along with the flies—the only person in the shop was the guide who worked there.

The guide's fly suggestion was #22 zebra midges in different colors, which I dutifully purchased to supplement the few I had left over from trips to New Mexico's San Juan River. His other advice was to stay in the section of river upstream of the public beach and the confluence of the nearly dry creek bed that bore witness to the muddy Paria River. Downstream of the Paria, bait fishing is allowed. Upstream from the confluence, the Colorado is regulated for catch-and-release fishing using barbless hooks. "The beach gets heavily fished by local worm anglers keeping whatever they catch," he told me. "They don't leave many trout."

I was not there to keep fish, and I was used to crimping my barbs, so his advice sounded good.

On that first of my two mornings at Lee's Ferry, since I had to check into the lodge and visit the fly shop, it was well after dawn before I was en route to the river. The eight-mile drive along Vermillion Cliffs to the river access was beautiful, though not as stunning as it would be that evening at sunset, or the next morning when I would make the drive at sunrise. It was also very foreign to the landscapes where I had spent most of my life. Vermillion Cliffs National Monument is aptly-named. Deep red canyon walls are punctuated here and there by towering rock pinnacles knifing the faded blue skies. Where the cliffs are not vermillion, they are horizontally layered and striated in patterns of brown, dark red, ecru, and mauve, broken up by signs of old landslides and glimpses of little slot canyons. Closer to the river, erosion has rounded the lower rock outcroppings, giving them the appearance of broken halves of giant beehives or wasp nests.

The Colorado River itself made for the landscape's starkest contrast. Immediately next to the river, the shore was lush, green and full of life. Yet just a dozen yards away it was cracked, caked, and brown: no visible blades of grass or leaves or flowers. Indeed, from the perspective of the access road up the hillside looking down toward the Colorado, the contrast was particularly sharp. Beyond a very narrow riparian corridor, the land all about looked as dry as fireplace ash.

Because, in fact, it was just about that dry. Annual rainfall at Lee's Ferry is only 6.99 inches. That falls well within the standard definition of a desert: a place receiving less than ten inches of annual rainfall. *Technically speaking, I was fishing for trout in a desert!*

As for the water itself, below the Glen Canyon Dam, though tinted aqua green, it is nonetheless quite clear as it flows over rounded multi-hued rocks that form an elaborate but not-quite-identifiable mosaic. This is not the natural state of the mighty Colorado. Two hundred years earlier at this time of year, the water would have been laden with silt brought downriver by the snowmelt on the slopes of the Rockies in Colorado. Since the building of the Glen Canyon Dam, however, all that silt settles out upriver in the reservoir. Downstream of the dam, the water looks purified.

All of which made for a stunningly beautiful—and unfamiliar—desert location in which to catch trout. The landscape took my breath away, and I could not help but be aware of it whenever I lifted my eyes. And yet, despite this beauty around me, I planned on fishing hard all day. I was there to cast flies and catch my first Arizona trout. Hopefully my first several. My concentration would be devoted to the river, and particularly to its fish and whatever invertebrate life it nurtured. No planned breaks except lunch and the necessary frequent drinks. I was alone, and hadn't thought there would be much else for me to do or see in the area.

Not that it was easy to forget I was in a desert. I didn't even need to open my eyes and look around at the beautiful desert landscape to know. Because by mid-morning, the air temperature was 109°. Even for summer in Lee's Ferry, that was relatively hot: about 9° warmer than the average high for June. And except for the early morning on my second day, when the nighttime cool of 80° lingered for a couple blessed hours after dawn, the temperature would remain that hot for most of the time I fished. Those were the hottest days I had ever spent fishing for trout, and remain so to this day.

To my thinking, a day *that* hot is a day for wet wading. I left my waders in my gear bag, stripped down to my swim suit and t-shirt, tied on a fly, and started out into the river.

Now I wet wade a lot in the chilly northeastern waters of New England, in air temperatures much cooler than 109°. In fact, I don't think I've ever *seen* temperatures over 100° in Vermont, which averages only about five days per summer topping 90°. By mid-June, and certainly in July, when temps may soar to a sweaty 85° in my home state, I've generally abandoned my waders in favor of shorts and sandals. So I couldn't possibly want waders in the hot desert air of Arizona. I'd melt in them.

But I was back out of that Colorado River water in less than fifteen minutes, with my legs numb from my thighs down. Lee's Ferry is about fifteen miles downriver from Glen Canyon Dam, which has a water depth of over 500 feet, and impounds Lake Powell, the second largest reservoir in the United States. One of the central realities behind this book, and one I will return to, is that water at the bottom of a deep lake—and thus water coming out of the bottom of high dam—is very cold.

The Colorado River, by the time it reaches Arizona, has also become quite large. Where I was fishing, it was about four hundred feet across, which is five to six times further than the longest casts I make with my 5-wt rod. The average June outflow is roughly 16,000 cubic feet per second (cfs). My notes for the day indicate the river current was moving at a brisk seven miles per hour. But the point of all these numbers is this: even fifteen miles downriver from a large bottom-release dam on a very hot sunny day, that volume of swiftly moving water is not going to warm up fast. The water temperature was only about 45° where I stood, which is considerably colder than the summer temperatures of my favorite New England rivers. No matter how hot the air, I wasn't going to be able to stand bare-legged thigh deep in that water and fish all day. I was experiencing a very classic southwestern trout fishing condition. And I was caught by surprise.

So what did I do? I put my chest-waders on, rolled them down to my belly, and worked my way back out into the swift current where I spent the day trying to find the right depth to balance the heating system with the refrigeration: the sweltering air and sun beating down on my shoulders with the frigid water tugging at my legs—all while simultaneously trying to position myself so that I could cast to where I might catch some trout. As noted, the river was several hundred feet across, and too swift and deep to wade out more than a fraction of that distance. I could fish only the one narrow channel along the near shoreline. I had to hope that at least some trout would be where I could reach them. Fortunately, since it was a barbless hook stretch of river, with catch-and-release regulations, and excellent trout habitat, there were plenty of fish to be reached near the shore.

There was no visible action on the surface—and the guide at the shop had said nothing about a hatch—so I decided to nymph. I fished with two flies: a bead-head hare's ear in a size #16 as my upper fly, and a the #22 zebra midge as a dropper. In the clear water and bright sunshine, with some of the fish presumably having been already caught and released by other anglers, I was expecting leader-shy trout. Between that and the small size of my flies, I was fishing 7x tippet: the lightest tippet I owned and the lightest available in most eastern fly shops.

Though I had never before waded a river the size of the Colorado at Lee's Ferry, I have fished many deep swift waters with nymph. I don't have any unique strategies of my own that I could market and sell in a fishing book. I have fished a so-called "Czech nymphing" approach with three flies, one of them on a sliding leader, but for the most part I use a very standard technique I learned from guides years ago and have been practicing all my life. I generally tie on two flies, the larger one on the end of my tippet, and a smaller "dropper" attached to the hook of first fly with an additional 18 inches of even lighter tippet. Depending on how heavily weighted the nymphs are, and how swift the current, I add enough extra weight to get my flies down quickly, and a strike indicator that serves as much to suspend the flies as it does to indicate strikes. It can be a very effective approach, especially when fishing close to your feet.

But while I appreciate the skill required in "mending" the line—flipping the loop of floating fly line either upstream or downstream of the strike indicator depending on the conditions in order to avoid drag and get the nymphs drifting naturally in a near perfect "dead drift" the way a real nymph would drift along with the current—the actually fly-casting of line with that many attached objects is not much fun. Indeed, there isn't much real *casting* at all. It is a method not-so-affectionately known as "chuck and duck," best suited for fishing water close at hand with little or no back-casting. The mechanics of "chucking" a big old split shot weight and strike indicator bears little resemblance to the romantic images of Brad Pitt's character, Paul, in the film adaptation of Norman Maclean's *A River Runs Through It*. The "duck" part comes from the number of times you whack yourself in the head, or hook your hat or ear, with all the heavy weights you are flipping about.

On this particular day, I simply did not want to fish that way. Part of it was the aesthetics. Chuck and duck, though effective, feels to me less like fly-fishing because it involves so little fly-casting. But also, on a river so large, I wanted the freedom to cast further out. So I eschewed the strike indicator, skipped the extra weights, trusted my eyes to pick up any strikes in the very clear water, and trusted my mending of the line to get a good dead-drift.

My approach proved moderately successful. Over the first day, sticking all morning to that same hundred yard stretch of river, I landed about one fish per hour, and hooked and lost a few others. They were typical rainbow trout in appearance, a little duller pink in their classic "rainbow" stripe than other 'bows I have seen, but still beautiful in their silvery sleekness. None were trophies; I didn't land any over sixteen inches. But like the peregrine falcons that have taken up residence on the cliffs of my hometown in Vermont, what they lacked in size and in vibrant color they made up for in athleticism. They were among the most acrobatic rainbow trout I've ever played. Most had in them at least three leaps, upwards of a foot out of the water, in the first few seconds after feeling the hook. A few broke my light line, and others spit out the tiny hooks, often in the midst of those acrobatic leaps.

It was hunger and thirst more than fatigue or midday heat that drove me out of the river for a lunch break that would be longer than I planned. Until I sat at the local restaurant—the one between the hotel and the fly shop—eating a burger and listening to the talk, I hadn't known that Vermillion Cliffs was an important home to endangered condors. The California condor, as I would learn over those two days, is a behemoth of a soaring scavenger. One can weigh up to twenty pounds and stretch close to ten feet from wingtip to wingtip, giving them the largest wingspans of any bird in North America. As one might expect from large soaring birds, they have slow metabolisms and can live fifty years or more. They usually don't even breed until the age of seven.

One of the few things my home town of Bristol, Vermont, has in common with Vermillion Cliffs is good habitat for endangered birds. For many years, Bristol Cliffs was one of only a handful of locations (other than zoos and aviaries) offering a chance of seeing the famed peregrine falcon. Among the fastest animals known, these raptors make up in speed and agility what they lack in wingspan. Similarly, Vermillion Cliffs was one of the few places where one could observe live California condors. By late last century, both the condors in the west and the falcons in the east were on the verge of extinction. In the 1980s, not a single breeding pair of condors remained in the wild. Survival for either species rested with visionary conservationists who had the plan of reintroducing the birds into the wild from captive breeding programs.

So, in a history not unlike that of the peregrines of my Bristol Cliffs, the final remaining wild California condors were captured for captive breeding. Making another connection to my home town, the work on condors was done by The Peregrine Fund, which established its condor breeding facility in Boise, Idaho. In 1996, they began releasing birds in northern Arizona where they could take advantage of cliffs and natural updrafts. The population has been growing since then. By 2006, there were about 250 condors back in the wild. Sixty of those resided in the Vermillion Cliffs area, each with a clearly numbered tag, visible from above.

And yes, it *was* possible to see these giant prehistoric birds *from above*.

I have a high endurance for fly-fishing, which is to say I don't get tired of it. I can cast sunrise to sunset on an Alaskan summer day. And I have. *Passionate* is the euphemistic term. *Addicted* may be a less positive but more accurate term to describe my fishing. Still, even when I was young taking five-day fishing-camping trips with my father to Maine's Allagash Wilderness Waterway, fishing experiences have also been about place. I want to know the trout I catch as part of the river they live in, as part of the land that river flows through, as part of the broad ecological community that lives in that land and that water. Though my work-related travel has enabled me to fish many places outside my home county, including in a few famous trout rivers, I don't want my experiences to become mere globe-trotting involving nothing but the size and number of trout that I catch, remembered with photos of fish that could have been taken anywhere. As I have aged, my desire to connect with the places I fish has increased. I wanted to cast flies at Lee's Ferry. I wanted to catch trout at Lee's Ferry. I also wanted to know Vermillion Cliffs and Lee's Ferry and the trout at Lee's Ferry as part of a landscape where California Condors are now living and reproducing.

And so, extending my lunch break, I stood atop the Navajo Bridge, five miles downriver of the actual location of Lee's Ferry and the campground and boat landing where I had been fishing. I was looking four-hundred and seventy feet down toward the Colorado River below, trying to avoid vertigo while watching three Condors alternately soaring below me and perching on ledges along the canyon. I spent half an hour with some tourists who had come just to watch the condors, and who cared nothing—and knew nothing—about the trout in the river below them.

Then it was back to fishing.

After a lunch break and condor viewing, I returned to the same stretch. Really, there wasn't anywhere else I could go except a hundred yards downstream into the short bait-fishing stretch I had been warned to ignore. Upstream was a deep box canyon accessible by boat only.

Downstream was more of the same. Lee's Ferry was the only access point to the river for several hundred miles—from Lake Powell all the way downriver to below the Grand Canyon—which was why John Doyle Lee started a ferry there in the 1800s. The afternoon fished much like the morning. I cast until nearly sunset when it was too dark to see my fly. Then with the red and orange sunset coloring the Vermillion Cliffs even more dramatically, I drove slowly back to Lee's Ferry Lodge for pub food and then bed, so I could do it again the following morning.

On the second day, knowing I would have to leave around 2:00 p.m. to start my drive back south to Sedona for the start of my conference, I got an even earlier start, hitting the river right at dawn with a plan of fishing through lunch without a break. I fished until noon with similar success: about a fish per hour. Then, just for the sake of exploration—and perhaps because the fishing was slowing down where I was—I worked downriver past the dry bed of the Paria River, out of the fly-fishing-only section of water, and to the beach where the guide had told me not to bother to fish and where I didn't really expect to catch anything, even though the water looked very nice there.

Like the rest of the river, the area was empty. One car pulled up while I was there and somebody took pictures. Nobody came near the water.

I hooked into a nice fish right away, landed it, and followed that almost immediately with a second, and then a third. It was the fastest action I had had in two days. So I stayed. I fished there for two hours and caught six fish, which were the six biggest of my trip. So much for the bait-fishermen cleaning the place out.

The drive down to Sedona that afternoon left plenty of time to reflect. I'd enjoyed a few firsts—and a few surprises. Those few dozen trout I caught over two days were my first Arizona trout. It was the first time I'd ever gone fishing *alone* outside my own familiar New England waters, without a friend or guide. Though as a child I'd caught rock bass, perch, and crappies in quarries of southern Indiana on hot July days, this was the first time I'd ever fished for trout in temperatures over 100 degrees. It was also certainly the widest river I had ever fished.

But the biggest surprise was that I'd had pretty nearly the whole place to myself. In a day and a half of fishing, I shared that stretch of river with only one other angler, and for barely more than an hour. On my first afternoon, a solo hiker had come through packing his rod. We chatted amicably. (I'd been fishing alone for so many hours with so much water that it may have been the first time in my life I was actually glad to run into another angler.) I told him what flies were working. He told me his name, where he'd hiked from, and where he was going next. But I forgot all those details. He watched me land a fish and took a couple photos for me with my camera. I took some photos of him, also with my own camera. Then we parted ways.

Also late on both mornings, an armada of huge rafts loaded into the river and floated past me making their way toward the Grand Canyon for a several-day trip—a trip I hope to do some day myself. But there was no fear of those rafts spooking my fish, or invading my privacy. I would have needed a telephoto lens to see the faces of the rafters on the far side of the river, and only indistinct traces of their voices carried over the rush and rumble of the mighty Colorado.

That experience will always be, for me, the epitome of southwestern trout fishing. Scalding hot air. An arid landscape I would have described as a desert—and which, indeed, technically was a desert. And a huge tailwater stretch of river. Even to this day it remains the icon and archetype of what I think of when I imagine southwestern trout.

Which is the great irony. For in thirty-five years of fly-fishing, no other experience catching trout in the southwest has ever been even remotely similar to that "archetypal" day-and-a-half in 2006, landing trout in the hot, arid Vermillion Cliffs with its vast leg-numbing river and dearth of other anglers.

Trout in the Desert

1.

Love and Trout in New Mexico

Summer, 1978; I had just turned fifteen. Many of the details—distances and travel times, exact dates, place names—have long since become blurry. Or else they simply weren't important at the time; perhaps I never even learned them in the first place. But the overall impression would last a lifetime.

I was in New Mexico, in the vicinity of Albuquerque where my family was visiting old friends. We took an overnight camping trip somewhere nearby. Surviving in my memory is a dim recollection of the name "Pecos Baldy," and there is a mountain by that name in the state park and wilderness area east of Santa Fe. Though only one of over a dozen 12,000 foot peaks in New Mexico, it is the major one around Santa Fe, so we were probably somewhere near it. But it was not the summit or the altitude I remember. In fact, I never even reached the summit, nor the small lake near the summit. What I remember was a little trout stream that flowed through the alpine meadow past our campsite in a bowl somewhere below the peak. It was there I had my first experience fishing a small, hike-in alpine water.

And I fell in love. I was only fifteen years old, as I already noted, but this was not a passing teenager's crush. It was a deep and abiding love that has proven itself over a lifetime.

Now I know what many readers think, probably with just cause. I was not even halfway through the adventure of being a teenage boy. Years of terror for parents and school teachers alike, and not a time when anything like true love happens. But I was not a terror. Though I hadn't enjoyed freshman year of high school any more than my three unpleasant middle school years, I was not a bad student, and I was certainly not a trouble causer. (At least not a regular one.) I was simply unpopular among my peers. Too bookish. Too good at math. Too interested in the outdoors. Not athletic. This combination of factors actually made me too unpopular to cause much trouble.

I enjoyed math and science and occasional opportunities to learn, but mostly I just endured school with all its bullying and meanness by day-dreaming my way through classes until I could get home. Once out of school, my fifteenth year became a time of wonder and exploration. Hopping off the school bus, I would dump my books inside and take off into the woods behind my house, exploring streams, building stick forts and dams, catching frogs in the swamp. Sometimes I didn't even make it past the stream at the start of our road where the school bus dropped me off; I'd leave my books on a bridge-side boulder and start following the water down into the woods. Or, reversing course, I'd meander my way upstream toward the boggy area between the ridges over the hill from my house. Or I'd just sit out on the old stonewall by the overgrown abandoned orchard across the street watching animals and imagining.

More than anything else, I spent time fishing.

I lived in the northeast of the United States, far from New Mexico, in a rural Massachusetts town of 800 residents. When my family moved onto a dead end road in the late 1960s, there was only one other house: a colonial farmhouse built in 1736 with a barn dating to 1810. We were surrounded by hundreds of acres of woods that had reclaimed old farmland and turned stone walls that once lined planted fields and pastures into mysteries. *Why is this stone wall out in the middle of the woods?* These were the days before the high-tech development boom of the 1980s hit the town, when some twenty or more houses would make our quiet cul-de-sac much less quiet, and block access to many of the acres of woods I had once roamed freely. Those early high school days were quiet ones, when all the woods were mine to play in.

I had already come to enjoy fishing in the old secluded bass pond over the hill and through the woods behind our house. Early on I mostly caught pan fish on a long cane rod without a reel, using for bait whatever I could dig up or pluck off the trees. Bluegill are not picky. If overturned logs and rocks did not reveal worms, bright red berries would often do the trick. But by the time I entered high school, I had begun to set my sights on more challenging targets: the largemouth bass that haunted those same waters. When my older brother landed a seven-pounder just short of two feet long, I abandoned the cane pole and pan fish altogether and began chasing the big bass with my closed-faced spinning reel and an assortment of Daredevil spoons, rubber worms, and surface plugs of the Hoola Popper and Jitterbug variety. And I was successful, too.

Annual wilderness camping and fishing trips to northern Maine with my father had also started when I was only eight years old. On these trips, catching wild brook trout by trolling streamer flies from a motorized canoe had introduced me both to cold water fisheries and to wilderness camping. Back home in my small Massachusetts town, even the small local trout stream that flowed out of our bass pond, under my road, and through several miles of then-undeveloped land had yielded a few fish for me, giving me the option to pursue trout or bass on those long Saturdays.

It was in the mountains of Colorado and New Mexico, however, far from the familiar streams and ponds of home, that a fifteen-year-old New England boy would first experience fly-fishing, and then a week later get his first taste of fishing a remote alpine stream. My father had a week-and-a-half of business meetings, first up in the mountain town of Granby, Colorado, and then down in Denver. So he made a family vacation out of it, and as a combined birthday present for the three of us, he hired a guide to take my two older brothers and me fishing for a day. It was my first experience with a professional guide. He got us into a mess of trout in the West Branch of the Colorado River. We caught rainbows and cutthroat, and even one small lake trout come upstream from a local reservoir. And all were taken on flies.

I still remember the flies. We used only two patterns all day. One was an Adams. The other was a Hornburg. The guide had tied one of each onto his line, and on his first instructional cast he hooked and landed two fish at the same time, one on each fly. Not a bad introduction to fly-fishing! Even the guide was surprised, and with a grin assured us that the occurrence was rare. But at that point, statistically speaking from own experience, fly-fishing yielded an expected two fish per cast. After that, every free minute of time during that family vacation was spent fishing. If my older brother didn't have a car to drive me down to the Colorado River, I fished the little mountain stream I could walk to from our lodge.

It was a week later that the business part of my father's trip ended and we made our way south to New

Mexico to see old friends and do a little camping and possibly some wilderness fishing. The camping trip almost didn't happen for me. The day we were to leave on the hike up into the Pecos area wilderness, I woke with a stomach bug. I lost the previous night's supper, and I couldn't hold down breakfast. I was heartbroken. I probably should not have gone on the trip, and I understood that. But I pleaded and begged and cried and whined. And my father and his friend yielded. My saving grace was that our host had two horses that were to be our pack animals, and given how light I was, I was allowed to ride one of them up the mountain along with our food and camping gear.

As noted, I don't remember many details of the trip. I am not even sure it was in the Pecos Baldy area. I think my older brothers were jealous of me, as they sweated and toiled their way up the mountain while I rode in comfort, plopped on top of a pack on top of a horse. (For the record, since I made it through the first day without losing the contents of my stomach, I was made to walk down the mountain on my own legs.) In any case, atop the packhorses I certainly was in a position to enjoy the beauty of the surrounding mountains.

Then we arrived at the camping site, and set up our tents in a meadow. The moment I had finished my duties I unpacked my little ultra light spinning rod. (I didn't own a fly rod at the time, but I would get one within a couple years.) The stream was one of the narrowest I have ever fished in for trout. I could jump or even straddle it in places. It carved a serpentine path through the soft meadow soil, almost as deep as it was wide, etching out big undercut banks. And it was loaded with little brook trout, ranging from four inches up to veritable monsters that sometimes topped seven inches. I spent all afternoon trying to catch them. We ate several for supper, fresh from the stream, fried in a pan over the fire, delicate and small enough they didn't even really need to be deboned.

At the time, because I was an easterner and because I was as yet unfamiliar with conservation topics such as "invasive species," the irony was lost on me: I was catching *eastern* brook trout, transplanted into the Rockies where they were apparently thriving. They looked just like the brook trout I caught in New England: dark green on the back, with their bright red and yellow spots on the sides. Perfect in their mystical beauty, but not belonging in that mountain stream in New Mexico.

The little stream behind the lodge where we had been staying in Granby also had eastern brook trout in it. Lots of them. They had heads too big for their bodies—or, rather, bodies too small for their heads, as though they couldn't get enough to eat. I wondered at the time if perhaps they had bred too well, and overpopulated the stream. But the real threat of the brook trout overpopulation wasn't so much to other brook trout as it was to the native cutthroat trout. I would learn many years later that introduced

8

species of trout have become a devastating problem for wild cutthroat trout in the Rocky Mountains. We were encouraged to keep as many brook trout as we could catch to get them out of the streams.

Growing up in eastern Massachusetts, where overfishing and farming had long ago eliminated native brook trout from most streams, I was used to fishing for stocked fish. Both hatchery strains of the indigenous North American char known as brook trout *(Salvelinus fontinalis)* as well as imported European browns *(Salmo trutta)* were planted annually in the streams of my home town. All the local trout fishing was of this "put-and-take" variety, completely dependent on hatchery support; it was not the presence of introduced brown trout that was the real threat to a healthy self-sustaining population of native brookies, but heavy fishing pressure and the degraded habitat that goes with development.

It was a different story for those streams I visited in the Rockies in the 1970s. They were my earliest experiences fishing for introduced species in what I considered to be "wilderness." At the time, I thought that any presence of trout, and thus any introduction of trout to any water at any time, was a good thing. I would only later learn the dangers of this kind of thinking. Cutthroat trout in the Rockies seem to be under attack from all sides.

There are three primary genera of fish popularly called *trout*, all within the *Salmonidae* family. The

Salmo genus contains various species and subspecies of European brown trout sometimes known as "true trout." Its only member native to North America are *S. salar*: Atlantic salmon including their landlocked strain, which are the state fish of Maine. Brown trout are easily bred in hatchery conditions, and can also tolerate lower quality waters where other trout cannot survive, and so they have been stocked successfully all across the continent. On many rivers, streams and lakes—east and west—they have thriving, self-sustaining populations. They also play only a marginal role in this book.

There are many members of char genus, known by its scientific name *Salvelinus*. Char are distinguished from true trout by having bright spots—yellow or red—on a dark background while trout of the *Salmo* genus have dark spots and a lighter background. Lake trout *(S.Namaycush)* and brook trout are the most famous eastern char, with brook trout indigenous from Georgia up through Maine and Quebec. Both arctic char *(S. alpinus)* and Dolly Varden trout *(S. malma)* can be found in the northwest, and are abundant in many rivers in Alaska. Rare, diminutive blueback trout *(S. alpinus oquassa)*, a subspecies of arctic char, still survive in a few New England lakes.

There are, however, very few indigenous char in the Rocky Mountains, and none in the southern Rockies. Native and rare bull trout *(S. confluentus)* do haunt a few of the coldest waters in the northern Rockies as well as the pacific northwest. They are voracious predators, dining on cutthroat trout—and occasionally surprising anglers as huge, three-foot long shadows emerging from deep pools to break a twelve or fourteen-inch meal off a light tippet. For all their rapaciousness, however, this one lone species of char native to the same Rocky Mountain waters as cutthroat trout have co-adapted with their prey. Bull trout and cutthroats have long cohabitated in a small number of the same waters. But neither brook trout nor lake trout are indigenous anywhere in the mountains of the west, and yet both—like the brown trout—breed well in captivity, and have a century-long tradition of stocking throughout the Rockies.

Members of *Oncorhynchus*, the third and final genus of trout have an evolutionary history tied to ancestors in the Pacific Ocean. The genus includes both rainbow trout *(O. mykiss)* that are native to the Pacific coast, and the many strains of cutthroat trout *(O. clarkii)* which at some point in their history made it eastward over the continental divide into the northern Rockies and from there down to the southern Rockies. The genus also includes the rarer Apache trout *(O. apache)*, Gila trout *(O. gilae)*, all five species of Pacific salmon found in North America, and steelhead (an anadromous strain of rainbow trout.)

And what do they have to do with cutthroat trout, in all its various strains indigenous up and down the Rockies? A great deal, as it turns out. Cutthroat have

11

been preyed upon, out-competed, and genetically diluted, throughout their home waters. Lake trout introduced into lakes and rivers of Wyoming and elsewhere in the Rocky Mountains, including the famed namesake river and lake of Yellowstone National Park, have devastated the native population of cutthroat trout through predation. By some reports, each lake trout consumes forty cutthroat trout a year. The problem with rainbow trout is different and in many ways far worse; as members of the same genus they are genetically close enough to the native cutthroat to interbreed with them, diluting and eventually wiping out the entire pure genetic strain of the native fish in waters where rainbow trout have been introduced.

As for brook trout I was catching in Colorado and New Mexico, the problem is competition. Dr. Kurt Fausch, a professor of fish, wildlife, and conservation biology at Colorado State University, has been studying and writing about trout for nearly 40 years. Fausch has noted that trout in general have "been introduced repeatedly almost everywhere that habitat was deemed suitable." Rainbow trout, for example, "are among the most widely introduced fish species in the world" having been stocked in ninety-seven countries, while brook trout are the second most widely introduced *salmonid*, having been stocked in at least forty-nine countries as of 2008. Having caught brook trout in the Pyrenees of Spain, I can attest to this. And, as noted above, I grew up as one of those people with the romantic notion that more trout in more water is always better. For sixty-five years from 1898 until 1963, the year I was born, between one and fifteen million brook trout were stocked in Colorado *per year!* And if I had been alive then, I would have been cheering on the stocking. The problem is that these brook trout eventually displaced the native cutthroats by out-competing them. As Fausch explains, brook trout "are now considered a major factor in the decline of most of the fourteen subspecies of cutthroat trout in the interior West. This is especially true for three cutthroat subspecies at the southern end of the species' range in Wyoming, Colorado, Utah, and New Mexico."[1]

Oddly enough, the same thing was happening the southern Appalachians, except brook trout were the victims: the native fish being displaced by stocked rainbow trout. One of the ironies is that eastern brook trout may actually be better adapted for some streams in the Rockies than are the native cutthroat, while western rainbows are better adapted for the southern Appalachians where brook trout are native. One important factor is spawning time. Rainbow trout and cutthroat trout spawn in the spring. Brook trout spawn in the fall. Fausch explains that rainbow trout are therefore better adapted to the rainy winters—and resulting winter floods—in the southern

---

1. Kurt D. Fausch, "A paradox of trout invasions in North America," *Biol Invasions* (2008) 10:685–701

Appalachians because that's what occurs in their native range in the Pacific northwest. Brook trout, by contrast, evolved with spring snowmelt floods, after their young have emerged. Winter floods scour brook trout eggs from the gravel, but rainbow trout spawn in spring, so none of their eggs are present in winter. Conversely, cutthroat trout at the southern end of their range in Colorado and New Mexico must contend with summer snowmelt runoff that can wash away their fry, whereas brook trout fry are larger by then and can handle it. Brook trout are thus pre-adapted for Colorado streams, as are rainbows for Georgia mountain streams. [2]

On that first trip to New Mexico, I probably did not know a cutthroat trout from a rainbow trout. I certainly would not have known a greenback cutthroat from a westslope cutthroat from a Yellowstone cutthroat. What I thought at the time was how beautiful and wild and scenic—and, well, *natural*—the setting was in the mountains east of Santa Fe. And it was all of those things. Even natural, in a way. What I didn't know was that the most enjoyable part of it for me, catching those "wild" brook trout, was the least natural part.

So what do I think now, some thirty-five years later? Was all of that stocking of brook trout in the Rockies over the first two thirds of the previous century wrong? Is all

2. Ibid.

stocking of all fish wrong? I don't think so. No more than turning soil and planting a garden, displacing some native plants with more productive ones. In some places where stocking happens, the native fish are no longer there. Brook trout simply can't exist in many rivers and streams in its native range. But brown trout can. In some cases, there never were any native fish. I have heard of lakes and streams in places like Wyoming's Wind River range that never had a native fish population. Fish simply never made it there. Yet the waters were capable of sustaining an abundant trout population. In other places, the introduced species find their own niche and coexist with the native species. Is it possible, then, that in many cases stocking fish, as a response, is a healthy solution and not the problem? Maybe it isn't even a terrible thing if some native fish have been displaced by another species that is better adapted.

However, what some of these experiences have ultimately suggested to me, at least, is that our race needs be a lot more careful about our constant and often arrogant engineering of the environment—especially just to meet our insatiable human appetites.

2.

From the Mountains to the Desert

Though one of my brothers eventually moved to Boulder, and I would fish Colorado many times over the next fifteen years, it would be closer to a quarter of a century before I would fish again in New Mexico. And in many ways my next experience in New Mexico could not have been any more different from my first.

Dave O'Hara grew up fishing the Catskills of eastern New York. We became friends fishing the trout streams of Vermont together in the spring of 1991 when he was a senior at Middlebury College and I was a second year professor there. The friendship solidified for the next few years when he married his college sweetheart, Christina, and remained in Vermont just two towns away. I explored more Vermont waters in a half dozen years with Dave than I have in the twenty years since then.

Dave and I would eventually write and publish three books together. For the third of these, *Downstream: Reflections on Brook Trout, Fly-Fishing, and the Waters* of

Appalachia, we would together explore streams and rivers up and down Appalachia, from Maine and Vermont through Kentucky, to southeastern Tennessee and western North Carolina. We have even fished together in Wyoming and Oregon (merely for the enjoyment of it, and not for any book writing).

It was to visit Dave and his wife that I returned to New Mexico. Dave left Vermont in 1998 to attend graduate school. He spent two years studying at St. John's in Santa Fe (and even did some professional guiding in the state.) My first visit to see him was in November—piggy-backed onto an academic conference in Albuquerque.

After some time with his family in Santa Fe, Dave and I did what Dave and I do: we hopped in the car and drove three hours west across the state to Bloomfield to spend an autumn weekday fishing the famed San Juan River.

Now New England, though loaded with thousands of good cold water fisheries, doesn't really have any single trophy trout water so famous that people from all over the world travel to fish there—places where the entire industry of a town is built up around tourist anglers. New England does have some wonderful brook trout and landlocked salmon fly-fishing-only waters to be sure, especially in Maine. A few, like Rapid River and the Magalloway, have some well-deserved notoriety. And one or two rivers like Vermont's Battenkill have historical significance and may elicit romantic nostalgia among fly-fishers. But they are nothing like the big famous western rivers.

The nearest thing we have is Salmon River in Pulaski, New York. Over the past two decades, it has become a world renown fall and winter fishery for salmon and steelhead which run up its dozen or so miles from Lake Ontario. During those runs, Salmon River offers combat fishing at its worst and best. But it sits five hours west of New England's "west coast," and it is a much more recent phenomena, one I had little experience with prior to my second visit to New Mexico.

All I had to prepare me for the San Juan were the several days I had spent on the Bighorn River in Montana. The little settlement of Fort Smith, three-quarters of an hour's drive upriver from Hardin, continues its existence for little reason other than the fishing on the Bighorn. Drift boat rentals, shuttle services, guide services, lodging, and fly shops right in Fort Smith, plus a few more lodges scattered along the river, are there because anglers travel there year round from all over the country—from all over the world—for the top-notch fishing and trophy trout. And they are ready to spend money.

Indeed, the Bighorn in Montana and the San Juan in New Mexico share many things in common, even though the former is in a state bordering Canada and its waters eventually find their way into the Atlantic, while the later, some 800 miles to the south, flows across a state bordering Mexico on its way to the Pacific.

The Bighorn was not "combat fishing" at its most intense. (Or at least it wasn't when I spent several days there in the 1990s, though I have heard it has gotten worse.) It wasn't combat fishing mostly because the river is inaccessible except by drift boat. The river flows through Crow Indian Reservation land. The only public access points are at the Yellowtail Dam where the river comes out of the Bighorn Canyon, where drift boats put in, then downstream at the five-mile mark (another popular place to launch boats) and twelve-miles (where the boats come out). Since almost all of the anglers are drifting the river, you generally don't see folks standing shoulder to shoulder tangling lines with one another. Granted, there is a fair bit of jockeying for position among boats, and some racing for favorite hot spots. Most guides get along fairly well with each other and share the river with mutual respect and not too much competitive angst. Others not so much.

The biggest similarity, however, is in the geography and character of the rivers. Both fisheries are so-called "tailwaters": stretches of river directly below bottom-release dams. Water is unique among liquids in that its densest temperature is not its freezing point; water is at its most dense at approximately 39° F (4° C). In other words, in winter the 39° water will sink below water that is colder (so that ice forms atop the lake rather than from the bottom), and in the summer the 39° water stays below the warmer surface water heated by the sun, providing a cool refuge for cold-water fish. In short, then, in a deep enough lake, the temperature at the bottom will remain close to a constant of 39° year round, which in turns means that water coming out of turbines at the bottom of a deep reservoir will also come close to 39° year round.

In the summer, if there is enough cold water coming through a dam, it will heat up only slowly, and may remain cold enough for trout and other cold-water fish for several miles downstream of the dam. This is true even in a very warm environment—even, as noted in the prologue, on a very hot summer day in a very dry climate. Combine this cold water with warm air, and you can get incredible conditions for a variety of aquatic insects. Of course, in the winter, this also means that the water below the turbines does not freeze as quickly, as it comes out a balmy 7° above freezing point. So fish have food in the winter as well as the summer. A big dam can thus create a superb cold water fishery in the middle of a hot dry climate where trout could otherwise simply not exist.

Tailwaters are thus the primary reason that one can find trout in the desert.

This describes both the Bighorn and the San Juan rivers, surprisingly similar rivers given their differences in latitude. In Bloomfield, New Mexico, thirty-some miles downstream of Navajo Dam where the blue ribbon tailwater stretch of the San Juan River begins, the average rainfall is a mere 9.32 inches—which technically makes the area a desert. That is only one-quarter of the annual rainfall we get in my home state of Vermont. The average daily high temperature in Bloomfield even in November is 56°. Hardin, Montana, forty-two miles downstream from the Yellowtail Dam and the blue ribbon tailwater stretch of the Bighorn is only slightly colder and less dry, averaging 11.99 inches of annual rainfall—barely outside the legal definition of desert—with average November highs of 48°. The July and August average highs in the two locations are even closer, with both towns hovering within a degree or so of 91°. [3]

But the main similarity stemming from the fact that both rivers are tailwater fisheries in warm dry climates is that they are both top-notch trout fisheries loaded with trophy trout which attract anglers from all over the country. And both fisheries are completely artificial; they are artifacts of human engineering: advantageous by-products of a dam whose purpose had nothing to do with fishing. To the angler fishing these rivers, it can be heaven. And standing in the river far enough downstream and out of sight from the dams, they even feel natural—as long as you don't think too much about it.

All of this I knew, but still nothing prepared me for the scene when I first arrived at the San Juan to fish. It

---

3. http://www.usclimatedata.com/climate. Accessed 1/22/2014.

was just before dawn. Dave and I had already stopped at a local fly-shop. We had been told to go with small midge nymphs, in hook sizes #22 or smaller. These are flies that will easily fit on my smallest fingernail. I never use flies that small except in very cold southwestern tailwaters like the San Juan or along the Colorado River in Arizona. When I tie flies, I don't tie sizes smaller than #16 because my fingers aren't able to handle movements that delicate. Furthermore, when fish are eating flies that small they are paying attention to very fine detail. Small flies require very light line. We would need to use the lightest tippet: a mere 7x or even 8x, which have a breaking strength of about two pounds or less. Hooking fish on tiny flies is a big enough challenge. Landing three to six pound fish in swift current on very light line is even more difficult.

Dave and I noted this aloud in the fly shop as we purchased the flies. The fly shop employee helping us with the flies—like nearly every fly-shop employee I have ever met—was himself an avid angler and occasional guide. He commented casually that he had been catching trout on size #30 flies. That silenced us. I have never even seen a size #30 fly. The entire fly was about the size of a barb on what I already think of as a small fly.

So down to the river we went, thinking about delicate fishing with tiny flies and light line. We parked at the lot in the popular hole in the fly-fishing only stretch. The fact that the lot was already crowded with cars should have tipped us off. We geared up and headed toward the river. Before we were even in sight of the main current of the river, we came to the edge of a pool about the size of a Little League baseball diamond. In that one pool, I counted thirty-two anglers casting. Thirty-two. I have spent five straight days fishing on great brook trout rivers in northern Maine and seen fewer than a quarter that many anglers—and that is in total during the entire period of several days. If there had been that many fielders in a baseball game there wouldn't have been a prayer of a baseball finding an opening. Even Little Leaguers, who can turn a routine grounder into a home run, could have defended the field with that many players.

The pool ranged from thigh deep to waist deep. It was wide and flat, and the water shallow and clear enough that we could see all the way across. There were a dozen or so monstrous brown trout cruising around the pool, all in plain sight of those thirty-two anglers. And with the anglers in plain sight of the fish, as well. I supposed that in the sunshine, the frigid water coming out of the dam flowed out into these side channels over the wide muddy flats and warmed up several degrees, perhaps getting from whatever frigid temperature it came out of the dam up somewhere closer to 55°—a temperature more ideal for trout metabolism. Or perhaps there was some abundant or larger insect hatching happening there in the warmer water.

These were just guesses. We did not stick around to find out. The brown trout in that pool were behemoths. Some were bigger than any brown I have ever caught—certainly fish that would attract my attention in almost any river. They were fish I would, in other circumstances, have wanted to cast for. But when we looked at the fish more closely, we could see that they were scarred, and many had splotches of white rotten flesh—a telltale sign of having been poorly handled: held by some angler with dry hands, that removes their protective mucus coating and leaves them susceptible to disease. Trout are beautiful fish, and they most often live in beautiful places. That is part of my attraction to them. But these were not beautiful trout. They were not the colors that anglers dream of, and painters and photographers try to capture to share in the pages of *Gray's Sporting Journal*. They were sad-looking fish. They reminded me of spawned-out, humpy salmon, a few hours before flopping up on a beach.

And for every fish we could see in that pool there were three or so anglers casting. It reminded me of a fish hatchery, or one of those stocked ponds where kids pay to dangle worms below bobbers. Except that these weren't kids fishing. They were adults, decked out in expensive fishing gear casting $900 rods. They had traveled from far afield. Some, we guessed from the languages we heard spoken, had come from Asia and Europe. They had paid quite a sum of money to be there casting for those fish.

This was my first real look at "combat fishing." Feeling a bit of disgust and dismay at both the crowds and the state of the fish, we ignored the siren call of the big browns, skirted the edge of the pool without taking a cast, and started winding through the brush down to the main river.

Amazingly enough, once into the cold swift current through the brush and out of sight a hundred yards upstream from that pool, we had the river almost to ourselves. There were no lazy behemoth browns cruising the shallows, so we had to work a lot harder. But eventually we did spot a number of eighteen to twenty-two inch rainbow trout clinging to the bottom of the river, knee- to thigh-deep in the current, occasionally rising a few inches off the bottom to sip midge nymphs drifting by. And so despite our initial bad experience in that pool, it turned into a very enjoyable day of fishing. It took me about three fish to adjust to the light tippet and the amount of pressure I could put on the line. Three fish in a row that broke me off in their first hard runs downstream. After that I started landing them. I lost track of how many I actually caught, but it was a fair number. Much of it was sight fishing: spotting a big rainbow in the current, and then working to get a perfect drift of a fly past its nose without spooking it.

We had only one other unpleasant experience that day. A guide with a client worked past us. That was fine.

The client landed a very nice trout. That was also fine. We enjoy watching other anglers land nice fish. The guide then proceeded to lift the fish and hold it out of the water for what seemed like at least five minutes, so that photos could be taken from every conceivable angle. In particular, the guide wanted to make sure there were several photos of him with the fish, and of him with each of the two clients and the fish, presumably for his future advertising. It was like being at a wedding where the photographer takes over, and keeps a hundred and fifty guests waiting while he or she spends an hour getting "perfect" photos of the bride and groom that will look good in his or her portfolio for future advertising. Watching the whole thing play out, we thought back on all the scarred, dying trout back in the pool with the thirty-two anglers. Now we understood why all the fish looked sick. They probably had been handled the same way, perhaps many times.

I have hired guides on several occasions in my life since that first day with a guide in Granby. And I have several close friends who are professional guides. My opinion of the majority of guides I know is high. They practice good fishing etiquette with respect toward other anglers on the river, as well as healthy conservation practices in their handling of fish, disposal of gear, use of boats, etc. Three days before writing this paragraph, I was steelhead fishing with a guide in Oregon. Even though we were his paying clients, and he might have considered that our satisfaction would directly impact his tip and possibly his future business, he did not let us fish near other anglers. I appreciated that. Even the guides I have met or witnessed who have been less polite have at least been conservation-minded in their choice of gear (using barbless hooks, for example), and in their fish-handling practices. Their livelihoods depend in some measure on maintaining a top notch fishery. This guide on the San Juan was an exception to our past experience. He may have thought he was helping his business in the short run by getting good photos. In the long run, harming the fishing harms the guides.

I have often wondered, since then. Does the sort of money involved in famous fisheries like the San Juan always have a sort of corrupting influence? I don't know. I don't know if it was a rogue guide, or part of the culture. I know that the San Juan, like the Big Horn, has a high density of big fish that can make for a thrilling day of fishing. It did make for a very nice day casting flies and hanging out with a good friend. But a problem with these blue ribbon rivers is that, in being everybody's river, they are also nobody's river. Fishing the small and not-at-all famous rivers around my home in Vermont, I can spend an entire morning without seeing anybody. But if I do see somebody, there is a mutual understanding. This is *our* river. Our *shared* river. It is our *home*. We are invested in it. And that shared investment fosters a sense of community and mutual protection for the home we share. The difference between seeing somebody on a river like that, even if you don't know them, and seeing somebody on a famous blue-ribbon stream where nobody lives within a hundred miles of the place, is like the difference between bumping into somebody in your small town post office and standing next to somebody on a crowded city subway. It is a sad reality, and the saddest part is that the better the fishing on a river is, the more it seems likely it will become like this.

I returned to the San Juan only one more time, while Dave was still a student at St. Johns. It was a Saturday in March. Perhaps because it was March and not November, or perhaps because it was a weekend rather than a weekday, the river was noticeably more crowded on our second visit. Even the main river had anglers spread out along its length (though not quite like the "combat fishing" in the flats, or in numerous salmon and steelhead streams around the country). We had to walk a ways to find a spot to fish. We caught some rainbow trout and enjoyed the day. But I would not return to the San Juan River unless I happened to be driving right past it.

3.

Texas and a Season for Trout

reg McNamee, in his beautifully written work, *Gila: the Life and Death of an American River,* makes an interesting comment about our use (or misuse) of the word "desert" to describe the Gila River, and lists several early names for the river that did not last. The etymology for its current name derives from either the Spanish word *hilar,* "to split," or from the Yuma Indian word *xila,* meaning "salty water running."

> The Gila has historically been one of the continent's preeminent desert rivers, but that word isn't quite right either. Desert: the English term and its Latin ancestors mean, at heart, an uninhabited or abandoned place, as in the 'desert isle' Robinson Crusoe found himself stranded on, a place given up as if depopulated after some terrible catastrophe. The Europeans who first saw the great arid expanses of northern Mexico and what is now the southwestern United States used a familiar term, ignoring the large populations of indigenous

Americans who made their home in the dry lands, as well as the astonishing variety of flora and fauna that have adapted to extremes of heat and lack of water, the preeminent characteristics of the region. [4]

Most of the major rivers that appear in the narratives of this book—especially the Colorado and San Juan Rivers, and the lower Gila Rivers —flow through expanses where, as McNamee points out, there is vibrant life. (Or there would be apart from human ravaging, overgrazing, and abuse and misuse of water.) They are not naturally desert-ed places, despite the implications of the word "desert." Vermillion Cliffs along the Colorado River, as I learned in my visit there, is a great habitat for California Condors. Not only do the cliffs and thermals provide the conditions for soaring, but there is enough life—and thus death—to feed these great scavengers. For example there is enough rodent, rabbit, and reptilian life in the area to support occasional cougars, bobcats, and foxes along with the ubiquitous coyotes.

Nonetheless these rivers are in very arid lands. They are also in lands that experience high summer temperatures and often lack the protective canopy of many rivers elsewhere in the country. In terms of rainfall

---

4. Gregory McNamee, *Gila: the Life and Death of an American River* (updated and expanded edition) (Albuquerque: University of New Mexico Press, 2012), 16-17.

and the technical definition, these rivers flow through deserts (whether the regions are named "deserts" or not). And, most pointedly, while they are indeed home to an "astonishing variety of flora and fauna that have adapted to extremes of heat and lack of water," with only a few exceptions they are not places trout would naturally survive except as artifacts of human engineering.

Nonetheless, one can find trout in the hot and arid southwest, as I have discovered on many occasions—and not only in the mountains and high altitudes of New Mexico and eastern and northern Arizona; I have caught more than a few trout in Texas.

There are, as it turns out, two ways to find trout in hot dry regions like most of the Southwest. One is find the right place: the tailwater from a large bottom-release dam. The other is to find them at the right time. There are several rivers in the south incapable of supporting a year-round trout population, and yet where trout are nonetheless stocked. They are stocked at the start of winter for a "put-and-take" fishery with the understanding that they will all be dead by the start of summer. Being cold-water fish, those that are not caught will simply die when the water gets too warm and low and oxygen-depleted to support them.

My first experience catching Texas trout was in a fishery like this. It was the Rio Frio—the "Cold River"—in Garner State Park in the hill country an hour and a half west of San Antonio. I visited there in March of 2008. As I have learned, this whole area of Texas has come to be known for what are called "exotics." This is not a reference to dancers in so-called (but very inaptly named) "gentleman's clubs," but rather to wild and unusual animals intentionally transplanted onto the local landscape from far away lands on other continents. They are transplanted specifically for the sake of hunting. But while they were often initially placed on controlled preserves surrounded by high fences where hunters pay a pretty premium for the privilege of shooting some animal that they would not otherwise see on the soil of Texas, in many cases these animals have escaped their confines and now roam freely. Some species have established self-sustaining populations, safe from whatever natural predators once hunted them in their native lands.

A classic example are the *axis deer*, which are natives of southeast Asia where their ancestors were once preyed upon by tigers. They were introduced to Texas in the 1930s, and have prospered since then. One brochure in Texas mentioned that axis deer could now be found in some twenty-seven different Texas counties. In many places they are pests. Garner State Park was closed for several weeks during January of that year to allow a special hunt of the overly abundant deer (since, thankfully, there were no Bengal tigers roaming the park to keep the herd thinned.) The park also had a population of exotic goats.

On our afternoon hike, we caught a good glimpse of what I think was a Catalina goat with its mixed white and black fur, light grey muzzle, and very impressive span of horns that would look good on a hunter's wall.

Though only imported from the west of our own continent, the rainbow trout of the Rio Frio fit that same category. In the rivers of Texas, it is an exotic. Stocked at the start of winter, they provide anglers of that hot state the chance to catch a cold-water fish that would not otherwise be found. Most are expected to be caught by the end of the winter. Those not caught? Chances of a rainbow trout surviving the summer in Texas are slim— even in a *rio* called the *Frio*.

Still. They are trout. And in a beautiful place. A March trip to an annual writers' retreat at Laity Lodge, a few dozen mile upriver from Garner State Park, provided the excuse and opportunity to take my wife to visit a quiet state Texas park during its off-peak months. And, of course, to catch a few trout. Which I did. My wife and I, and our friend Lolene, who had driven over from Houston to join us, arrived a little after dusk. We wandered through the park and its nearly empty campgrounds to find our rented cabin, unpacked, shared a late meal, and went to bed. In the morning I rose before dawn, donned my sandals and shorts, and stepped out onto frost-covered ground and into the crisp morning air for a bit of fishing while the women slept in.

Where I first hit the river, it was shallow and gravelly, with no pools and no obvious structure for a fish to hold. I knew March was late for the winter trout season. Despite the frost that kept me shoving my hands in my pockets for snatches of warmth, summer was coming, and the famed bell was tolling for these trout. Stocking was long since finished for the year. Any fish in the river had been targeted for months by anglers seeking to catch with no intention of releasing. I moved quickly upstream, looking for decent water where a fish might hold out.

It took me about an hour to find some good water: pools and overhanging banks and something less uniform than the beach where I'd started. I soon hooked my first fish. And then my second. To be honest, although they were my first Texas trout—and as far as I knew at the moment, they might be my last—I don't remember much else about the fish themselves. They were slightly pasty and nondescript stocked rainbows of a little under a foot in length. I don't even remember exactly how many I caught. It was at least two. It was no more than six.

What I do remember was coming to a bend in the river just as the sun peeked out over the hill to the east. The day had dawned several minutes earlier, and I'd been watching the golden morning light strike the hilltop ahead of me and slowly move down the slope. But now the sun was high enough to peer at a low angle over the hill behind me with the promise of warming my back and melting off the frost. And in that light and promise of heat I came to the bend, stepped through a row of bankside trees, and saw a herd of the axis deer just across the river grazing in a clearing. There were about a dozen of them, spotted not unlike a whitetail fawn in the northeast. Except these were mature deer, including several proudly-antlered bucks. They were aware of me, and the closest few turned and began moving slowly away. But they weren't spooked like the whitetails on my own property would have been if I had stumbled on them in the woods.

I stopped fishing for a while and watched them. Not long after that, I returned to the cabin for some breakfast and instant coffee. Though I had several hours to spend in the park that day, I didn't bother fishing any more. Some part of my brain was speaking to me in critical tones. *Trout don't belong here. They can't even survive the summer. This is just a put-and-take fishery. Between fishing pressure and the challenges of survival for a trout in Texas, very few of these fish will be alive at the end of the summer.*

The reality, however, is that much of the fishing in my home state of Vermont is not all that different from the scene at the Rio Frio in Texas' Garner State Park. Thousands of trout are stocked each year in the New Haven River (two and a half miles north of my Vermont house) and the Middlebury River (six and a half miles south). Brook trout are stocked in the upriver portions. Brown trout and Rainbow trout—which are not native anywhere in the state—are stocked in the lower portions. A few days after the stocking trucks leave, the anglers will start hitting the river hard. And with great success. These newly stocked fish, fresh from the hatchery raceways, are none-too-smart. When an angler walks to the bank with a rod, they practically swim over waiting to be fed. Fish by the creel-full will go home to the freezer and frying pan. In Vermont, it is winter and not summer that is the difficult season for trout survival. So the state stocks at the start of the summer with the knowledge that not many of those fish will be around when the ice melts the following spring. Other than that, the practice is quite similar.

I have read that at one time Texas did have a few rivers in the Trans-Pecos range with a native population of Rio Grande cutthroat trout, but they had been extirpated from the state more than a century ago, leaving Texans without opportunity to enjoy the beauty of any species of trout in their own state. So I can't begrudge the residents of the Lone Star State their own chance to pursue the cold water species I love so much, nor criticize their efforts as any less natural than the conditions leading to most of my own fishing for stocked rainbow and brown trout that in most places throughout Vermont have replaced the native brook trout. And in some way, I know, the rather unnatural fishery in both states not only brings delight to many, but also puts many people in closer contact with nature than they would otherwise be.

In any case, as I would learn not too many years later (and not too far away from the Rio Frio) Texas *does* have some year-round trout fishing.

The seasonal presence of trout on a few miles of the Rio Frio notwithstanding, if I had been asked in 2010 to name the state with the largest chapter of Trout Unlimited (TU), I would never have guessed Texas. My first few instinctive guesses would have been Montana, Idaho, or Wyoming because of their famed trout waters. If I had been reminded of the low population densities of those states, I might have changed my guess to California which has both some fantastic trout fishing in the mountains and also a lot of cities. The city of Sacramento could certainly support a large TU chapter devoted to the river of that same name and all its tributaries. Or I might have guessed Colorado, thinking it would be a TU chapter on some river in the Denver area. Or it could be Michigan, with its famous trout streams not too far north of the major city of Detroit. Or Oregon. Or Washington. Or Maine. Or New York.

Texas might not have been the last state I would have guessed, but it would have been in the final ten. Yet the largest chapter of Trout Unlimited, with roughly 5,000 members, is the Guadalupe River chapter in Texas. In January of 2013, I had a couple of mornings to pursue trout on the Guadalupe with two different officers of the GRTU: Rafael Torres, the then vice-president of

Chapter Affairs, and Jimbo Roberts, the vice-president of Fisheries. Those experiences on the Guadalupe were as different from the Rio Frio in March as the Rio Frio was from the rivers of New Mexico or Arizona. But those few hours of casting flies for trout left me with considerable appreciation for the river, for the passion and knowledge of the anglers who pursue trout there, and for the efforts of the GRTU to produce an excellent "cold-water" fishery in a rather unexpected place.

The Guadalupe carves its way through limestone out of the Texas Hill Country northwest of San Antonio. Its famous native fish is the Guadalupe bass: the Texas "state fish" which can be found only in the Hill Country. Upper portions of the river still provide excellent bass fishing. But in 1964 the Army Corps of Engineer completed the world's largest earthen-works dam, impounding the Guadalupe and creating the roughly eight-thousand acre Canyon Lake.

Now the dam and its impoundment are dwarfed in all respects—height of dam, volume of water, area of the lake—by Lake Powell and the Glen Canyon Dam. Still, for an earthen-works dam it is impressive. And at a hundred and twenty-five feet deep, the dam also created a nice tailwater, cold enough that it now provides the southernmost trout fishery in the United States.

The trout are not native there, of course. How they arrived is an almost humorous story I learned from Rafael and Jimbo. Apparently some 10,000 trout were first stocked there by the Lone Star Brewing company—with the approval of Texas Parks and Wildlife—for a one-time event and seasonal fishery. Large numbers of anglers arrived to catch the fish, and large numbers of fish went home on stringers. But it turned out that the habitat was actually hospitable enough for rainbow trout that some of them survived the summer thanks to the cold water from the bottom-release dam. And thus was born a year round trout fishery in Texas: the southernmost trout fishery in the United States.

In winter months, there are more than fifteen miles of trout water below the dam. The bottommost several miles, like the Rio Frio, are seasonal trout waters. In the summer, the amount of trout habitat varies depending on flows. In dry years, the flows coming out of the dam are a mere 90 cfs—about one twentieth of what comes through the Glen Canyon Dam in the month of June. Even then, the upper five miles provides year-round trout habitat. In moderate years, when flows remain over 250 cfs, trout will summer-over for ten or more miles downstream of the dam. And on high flow years the entire fifteen miles of river can hold trout throughout the year.

Though most of the land along the river is private, as of 2013 the GRTU had leased eighteen access sites over those fifteen miles (and they were working to gain more). Seven are open year-round, the rest only in winter fishing months. (In the summer months, the river is a popular destination for inner-tubing and the local economy revolves around non-angling forms of water recreation.) The state also maintains five public access sites where visiting anglers can fish. And, like in Vermont, the law allows an angler in the river to wade upstream or down, as long he or she keeps a foot in the water, or stays below the mean high water mark of March.

The river is well-stocked throughout the winter by the state, and the GRTU aids in the efforts—including the use of Whitlock-Vibert boxes which allow trout eggs to hatch in the river, protected, until they develop through their smolt stage and swim free. Indeed, under the loving and knowledgeable care of folks like Jimbo and others at GRTU who promote conservation efforts, the river has become a really fine fishery. So there were plenty of trout to be caught. And good-sized ones too.

Fishing a pair of nymphs (with patterns unique to that river), I landed a half dozen fat rainbow trout, and watched my hosts reel in a few more (when they weren't showing me around.) The typical Guadalupe rainbow measured sixteen or seventeen inches, and the two largest were at least twenty. These were much bigger than the rainbows I was catching on the Rio Frio.

It was a surprisingly beautiful place to fish, also. Below the dam (which sits at an altitude of roughly nine hundred feet), the river cuts and winds through bluffs as it makes its way toward the small city of New Braunfels, about half an hour northeast of San Antonio. It is a picturesque southwestern landscape, and one of very few rivers in which I have ever been able both to catch trout and to look up and see cactus growing on the ledges above me. Though in places the banks are lined with homes and camps, there are numerous stretches with no signs of human habitation. Raising my eyes above the water, I could see through towering bald Cyprus trees lining the back, up steep riverside bluffs, and higher to the occasional osprey soaring overhead.

Though we did not have the river to ourselves, it was certainly not crowded. The few anglers we met were cordial, and respectful of each others' space. The GRTU, despite its size, was clearly a community of anglers who got along well with each other, and had a common bond of enjoying the fishing and protecting and improving the fishery. In other words, it was altogether different from the combat fishing on the San Juan in New Mexico where everybody seemed to be strangers to one another. While I harbored no great desire to return to the San Juan— regardless of the wonderful numbers and size of the fish there—as soon as I left the Guadalupe I wondered when I might return there and cast again. And not just for the trout. I'd also like to get up above the lake and catch some of the native Guadalupe Bass where the river is less impacted by human engineering.

But on that first trip, I was happy just to be able to stand in a river in January (without a winter coat or gloves), to make a couple of new friends, and land a few trout on a fly in a surprising place—a place where trout, with a bit of help, have managed to survive an environment otherwise quite inhospitable to their kind.

4.

Gila Trout

There is something which unites magic and applied science while separating both from the 'wisdom' of earlier ages. For the wise men of old the cardinal problem had been how to conform the soul to reality, and the solution had been knowledge, self-discipline, and virtue. For magic and applied science alike the problem is how to subdue reality to the wishes of men: the solution is a technique; and both, in the practice of this technique, are ready to do things hitherto regarded as disgusting and impious.

—C. S. Lewis, *The Abolition of Man*

The landscape around me looked ravaged. It was late in March, 2014. We had been driving across Texas on I-10, making our way from San Antonio to Gila Hot Springs, near the Gila Cliff Dwellings National Monument in the Gila National Forest in southwestern New Mexico. Our plan was to spend three days fishing the three main headwaters of the Gila: that is, the three that bear the name *Gila:* the aptly named West Fork, Middle Fork, and East Fork of the Gila River. But it is an eleven-hour drive from San Antonio, even at the speed limit of 80 mph. After I gave an early Monday evening reading from my medieval historical novel, *The Rood and the Torc,* we managed two and half hours of driving the first night. But we still had a long drive ahead of us. Tuesday morning we checked out of a clean but generic interstate hotel in Sonora and were on the road by 8:00 a.m., hoping to be into Gila Hot Springs by supper.

I was traveling with my friend Phil Broderson, who had driven his Nissan Murano down from Oklahoma to meet me for the trip. We have one of those modern technology-enabled friendships that would not have happened twenty or even ten years ago; we were introduced via Facebook by a mutual friend, and discovered we shared common interests in acoustic music, the writings of C. S. Lewis, and fly-fishing. We corresponded via Facebook for a couple years before meeting in person in January of 2013 at a weekend conference in the Texas Hill Country. It was the only time we had met in person before taking this trip together a year later.

It was a hot drive and we needed the air conditioning. At home in Vermont, we still had two feet of snow on the ground, with temperatures down to 0° at night. Here in Texas, the temperature registered at 84°. I was very aware of that, because the transmission on Phil's car died mid-morning, leaving us stranded in the small city of Fort Stockton—a city with no Nissan dealer and no car rental company. After five hours of waiting, we were finally towed eighty-five miles up to Odessa where there was a dealer who could repair the car, and, equally importantly (to me), pick up a rental to continue our trip.

Eight hours later, and several miles further away from our destination, we were once again heading west, now on I-20 looking to merge with I-10. This is the west Texas "desert." It can be beautiful, I know. But everyplace I looked—over tens of thousands of square miles in every direction—the landscape was dotted with oil pumps, one after another, their famous arms slowly rocking up and down. Besides the wells themselves, there is all of the supporting infrastructure necessary to use those pumps to extract the oil from the ground: pipelines, gravel access roads, outbuildings, occasional drilling rigs, and lots of fencing. All for the purpose of sucking fossil fuel from the ground to keep our cars and trucks rolling, and fueling the economy that makes us a rich and extravagant nation.

Along the back roads off the interstate, it looked even worse. The operator of the flatbed truck talked some about the industry as he drove us (and Phil's Murano) from Fort Stockton to Odessa. He spoke with appreciation of fracking, and how all the oil now available through that technology had the local economy booming once more. His towing business was doing quite well as a result; the harsh desert conditions and less-than-careful driving had the oil company rigs and other service vehicles breaking down with regularity. He hoped to make a whole bunch of money in a short amount of time so he could open a restaurant.

But I could only listen with a sick heart to his talk of fracking. I looked at this ravaged landscape and the wounds that the insatiable appetites of our race have caused—above ground, below ground, to the ground water, plants, birds, and animals, and to each other—and wondered if it could ever heal. Maybe when a thousand years have passed and the broken-down pumps have rusted away to nothingness.

The reason I was on my way to the Gila was in part to look for some Gila trout, and to see the places where they lived. I wanted to experience once again some high alpine wilderness in the southwest. Thirty-five years earlier, I had caught eastern brook trout in the mountain streams in the Pecos range east of Santa Fe. That setting, as I noted earlier, had a profound imaginative impact on me. It brought pure delight to a young heart and mind. Cold mountain streams have ever since held a preeminent place in my angling heart.

But so far all the trout I had ever seen in the southwest were the result of some form of human engineering. They were introduced fish. In some places, a thriving, healthy, self-sustaining population. In most places, though, they were dependent on stocking. In some they were seasonal, only capable of surviving the winter. Or they survived thanks only to human edifices—the massive dams that have so impacted the southwestern landscape.

However there are native trout in the arid southwest. They live high in the mountains, often at 6,000 or 7,000 feet in elevation, in waters fed much of the year by snow runoff, and by cold springs exposed tens of thousands of years ago by volcanic eruptions like the ones that created the caldera from which the headwaters of the West Fork of the Gila flow. They remain shielded by a canopy of forests that grow even in the southwest at altitudes where peaks can trap passing moisture.

Many of these trout populations are gone, mostly because of human changes to their environment. But endangered remnants of some remain, where they and their environment have been protected. Strains of native cutthroats can still be found in the higher elevations in tributaries of the Rio Grande near the border of Texas and New Mexico. There are even trout in the mountains further south in Mexico. Among all these desert trout, the Apache and Gila trout of western New Mexico and eastern Arizona—golden-hued relatives of the rainbow trout—hold a special place in my imagination. I had never caught or even seen one.

For the past few weeks, as I prepared for the trip, I have been reading Greg McNamee's account of *Gila: the Life and Death of an American River*. It is a beautifully written tale, but also a tragic one, recounting some of the more extreme atrocities that humans are willing to commit upon one another and on the earth. It is a tale of a river that once sustained an abundance of life—including human life—over tens of thousands of square miles from the mountains of what is now New Mexico for six hundred miles westward to the Colorado River. And which now is just a dry river bed for much of its length.

Growing up in the northeast, where water is abundant, it is hard for me to imagine that a once swift and abundant river like the Gila could be so dammed and exploited that its waters no longer reach the ocean. But, of course, the Colorado River itself no longer reaches the ocean much of the year.

At its headwaters in the national forest that bears its name, however, the Gila still flows year round, clean and clear and cold. It has been offered some protection, thanks in part to the efforts of Aldo Leopold. Which was another reason for me to visit. I had taught courses at Middlebury College exploring the writings and ideas of Leopold, whose life was shaped in part by his experiences along the headwaters of the Gila and by the beauty of that area. I wanted to see this land that so inspired and shaped one of our country's most important conservationists.

I also wanted to find some reason for hope. And I did. I succeeded both in finding hope in the headwaters of the Gila, and in delighting in the beauty of one the country's great natural treasures. I just didn't succeed in catching any Gila trout. Though not for lack of trying.

When I started planning the trip, I had expected catching Gila trout would be a challenge. The stretches of tributary waters managed as wild fisheries are open only for limited periods for catch-and-release fishing with barbless hooks. I did not visit during one of those times, and so I had to fish in hatchery-support stretches. This was disappointing since I was interested in wild desert trout. Still, visiting the Gila River and seeing—much less actually catching—any Gila trout had seemed worth the visit. The problem was that the stretch of river we fished had been ravaged by a series of natural disasters.

The first was the famous Miller Fire of April and May, 2011. The fire primarily impacted the West Fork, and the very lower end the Middle Fork. The fire burned off about 88,000 acres. Then came the even more devastating Whitewater-Baldy Fire that started in May of 2012 and continue through July. It was a running crown fire, leaping and torching through a mixed conifer forest of spruce and fir. Consuming some 298,000 acres, it was the largest wildfire in New Mexico state history, impacting all of the headwaters of the Middle and West forks above Gila Forks—the exact area we had planned to fish. In addition to destroying the cottonwood gallery between the Middle Fork and the East Fork, it also dumped a tremendous and deadly volume of ash into the water. Finally came the Silver Fire in the summer of 2013. Though it did not reach the West and Middle Forks, it did impact the Gila River watershed as it burned about 140,00 acres of pinyon-juniper scrub at elevations from 6,000 feet up to the mixed conifers at 10,000 feet.

And then, following three consecutive years of tremendous wildfires came the tremendous flood of September 2013—just a few months before my visit, but weeks after the trip was carved into my calendar and the planning had begun. The combination of fire and flood was doubly devastating. In terms of the fishing, it was a combination that did me in. Though the Ponderosa pines on the hillsides and further up from the river are well adapted to surviving and even thriving in forest fires, the cottonwoods along the riverbank are not. They were almost entirely destroyed by the fire: burned, killed, and left dead. Then it started raining. In the town of Gila, many miles downriver of Gila Forks, the average flow during the six or so weeks of spring runoff in March and April is 300 cfs. That is the volume of water during *high* flow of the spring floods when snow is melting in the mountains. In the summer the average flow is only about 120 cfs. During the September flood of 2013, in the town of Gila the Gila River was carrying 30,000 cfs. That made it the third highest flow ever recorded. In that raging torrent, all the debris from the fire was swept downstream in a torrent leaving the valley floor looking like a war zone.

John Kramer, from the U.S. Forest Service at the Gila National Forest, explained the three-fold punch of that fires-followed-by-flood event. First, in the high-severity burn areas along the West Fork, the fire had destroyed much of the vegetation and duff layer that once served to intercept, absorb, and hold water. The result was the near record amount of water in the river. Second, a tremendous amount of black ash was actually *in* the river, smothering and killing aquatic life on a grand scale. Finally, the dead trees—particularly the cottonwoods—were swept into the river, and their tumbling action added to the scouring effect. Prior to the fire and flood, the river valley along the West and Middle Forks had been lush and green with brush and grass and heavy vegetation.[5] When we arrived, a few months after the flood, it had been scoured of vegetation—and was littered with flood debris. It looked almost barren. Apparently the state biologists in charge of stocking also saw the same devastation, for the river was not stocked there that year.

---

5. John Kramer, personal interview, April 12, 2014.

This complete story of flood devastation I did not hear until some time after my visit, but I did hear enough from folks I talked with before my visit to know that fishing prospects were grim. I suppose one response would have been not to fish. But another approach was to fish long and hard, and to attempt to make up for a scarcity of fish with an abundance of effort. Phil and I planned to fish breakfast to supper and cover as much water as we could over three days in the area known as Gila Forks, where the three main branches come together. We thought that if we got far enough upriver into the wilderness, we were bound to find at least one trout that had survived.

On the first day, we fished our way three miles up the Middle Fork, starting at 9:00 a.m. and not getting back to the car until 6:00 p.m. When we quit fishing, it took us ninety minutes to hike back to the car at a steady pace, following the streamside trail at times, walking riverbank at times, and wading only when we had to.

We did not catch a single fish. It is possible we did not even see one, though the final hole I fished—the farthest upstream point I would reach on the Middle Fork, late in the afternoon—I thought I saw one trout flash at a fly and catch the hook for just a second before it was gone. That was the only hint of a Gila trout that day. We did, however, see a good afternoon hatch of small black stoneflies. For two to three hours in the middle of the afternoon, they were coming up steadily off several gravelly riffs, crawling on rocks, swarming in the air, and landing on our legs. In a few places we also saw significant numbers of caddis larvae encased in beautiful coats of multi-colored pebbles. Whatever damage the fire and flood had done to the trout population, at least two species of macro-invertebrates were recovering nicely.

On day two, we dropped down a few miles to the confluence with the East Fork. In the morning we fished upriver on the main stem for a mile or more. After lunch, we fished the East Fork as far up as we could until we hit private property. And, in fact, since we were wading upriver where there were no posted signs, we actually unwittingly fished well past the private property boundary, only learning our mistake when we climbed out of the river onto the dirt road and started walking back downstream. We saw no trout and no caddis casings. There were a few black stoneflies, but nothing like the day before.

What we did see was a considerable amount of silt and mud in the water. It wasn't so muddy as to be unfishable, but visibility was not much more than two feet. I wondered what caused it. It had not rained. There was little or no snow left to melt, and neither of the other branches had shown signs of silting. There is still a considerable amount of mining in the surrounding mountains, but I was told there were no mines upstream on the East Fork. I thought I had an answer when I saw that a private road crossed the river several times—and as we were fishing our way upstream we watched a car drive through the river at one of those crossings churning up the bottom. But upstream of all the crossings, the water was just as muddy and off-color. Eventually, on private land upstream of the National Forest boundary, we came upon a small ranch with several head of cattle and fences that ran down to and across the water. Certainly a large heard of cattle trumping in the water over a long period could muddy it up. But we saw no sign of cattle actually in the water. Was somebody building a new road upstream? We never solved the riddle.

Day three was my longest day yet. I began the morning fishing from just below the Cliff Dwellings all the way downriver to the confluence with the Middle Fork. The morning temperatures each day were barely above freezing according to our car thermometer. It felt that cold. And at 8:30 a.m., the water temperature on the West Fork was 44°. This was not wet wading weather. And so, like the previous two days, I started in long sleeves and fleece. By late morning, however, the air temperatures had risen to very comfortable t-shirt weather, perhaps 75° or so. I walked back up the road, sweating profusely in my waders in the hot New Mexico air, and feeling foolish each time a car drove by.

Phil and I took a lunch break and did the tour of the Cliff Dwellings. By then Phil had perhaps had enough fishing. His legs were sore, and we had gone two and a half days without a bite. More importantly, though, he had to find some internet service back at Doc Campbell's Outpost so he could get some news about his car, and when it might be repaired. But I was as yet unwilling to give up. I have had the occasional day in which I fished and caught nothing. On rare occasions—primarily winter or early spring fishing—I have even gone two days without catching anything. I don't know that I have ever in my life fished three long days without landing a fish. The thought that this might happen, especially since I had shared with several angling friends my expectation of catching my first Gila trout, did not set well with me.

So I pressed on alone. For the first time in three days, I took off my waders and went with sandals, shorts, and a t-shirt, and slathered myself in loads of sunscreen to protect against the power of the sun at high altitude and thin air. And then, just as we had done on the Middle Fork, I fished my way upriver on the West Fork three miles. Or, rather, I hiked upriver two miles as quickly as I could in hopes of reaching some stretch of water that might have less fishing pressure, and thus might be less dependent on stocking and less impacted by the flood. Then I fished upstream another mile from there, casting a whole assortment of flies ranging from size #18 midges and small attractors up to size #8 stoneflies and wooly buggers. I cycled back through flies I had tried the previous two days. I tried new flies. I fished with weights. I fished without weights. Nothing worked. Not even a hint of a fish.

And then, in almost the last hole I fished, a good three miles upriver from the car and across the wide caldera of some ancient super volcano, just before I had to start back downriver to meet Phil for our long drive to Phoenix, I finally saw my first two Gila trout. They were unmistakable, at the bottom of a deep hole, hiding under a fallen tree. I saw them only because I snagged a pair of nymphs in the tree, and thought I might wade out to recover my flies. I can be almost as stubborn about saving flies as about avoiding getting skunked. As I stood staring into the depths of the pool, pondering the fact that it looked about as deep as I was tall and wondering to what lengths I was willing to go to save a pair of flies I had tied, I saw the fish move. First one. Then another. The first was about 11 inches and the second a bit smaller: perhaps 7 or 8 inches. I could feel the adrenaline surge. The sudden quickening of my heart.

I backed away from the pool and half-heartedly fished my way upstream another hundred yards or so, just to give the fish twenty minutes to unspook. Then I returned and gave them my last and best effort. I spent thirty minutes trying to drift flies down into them, where they sat below one branch and behind another.

Between the swirl of current below the drop-off, and the obstacle of those trees, it was not an easy drift. I lost more flies. Still, I managed on a couple occasions to put a fly in front of their noises. But they were obviously spooked by then. They were not budging. Eventually I left in defeat.

><+>-O-<+><

In the final chapter of *Gila*, titled "Regaining Paradise," McNamee writes one of the most haunting, insightful, and moving paragraphs of his book.

> For the most part we know the rivers of the desert only by their absence, only as tiny blue scratches, separated by ellipses, on highway maps, in the cartographic code for the dead. The desiccated beds of those once great rivers, spanned by unsteady bridges, mock their intended function, carrying runoff from the heavens only a few days of the year, effluent from sewage-treatment plants with greater regularity. For the rest of the year, bone-dry, they serve as drag strips for three-wheeled recreational vehicles, as dumping grounds for unwanted mattresses and pets, for defaulting drug dealers. They are rivers in name only, an insult to the theory and practice of flowing water. [6]

---

6. McNamee, 174.

But then he follows that up with a promise of hope. A glimpse, perhaps, of why he wrote the book.

> To bring back the old rivers is not an impossibility; to declare that time cannot be reversed is mere dogma. But to regain the Gila, the Colorado, the San Pedro…will require an absolute change in the politics and economics of the American West, away from the ceaseless rapacity that has characterized the last century and toward a more sustainable ethic, one that recognizes water as the best of all clean industries, the best, as Heraclitus says, of all things.[7]

I grew up spending time in and around the Androscoggin River in Maine. Though like most rivers in New England it has been dammed, it is not a river that has ever been in danger of being bled dry. It was, however, a river that could well have been pronounced dead. In 1972 it was labeled by *Time Magazine* as one of the ten filthiest rivers in the United States. As I have recounted in a previous book (*Downstream: Reflections on Brook Trout, Flyfishing and the Waters of Appalachia*) the Androscoggin has been brought back to life. It is no longer a dumping ground for raw sewage and the chemical outflow of paper mills. I found hope back in the late 1990s when I caught

---

7. Ibid.

my first brook trout in its waters near the border of Maine and New Hampshire. The river is by no means fully restored. It is still plagued by development, agricultural runoff, and a host of other problems. But it is immeasurably healthier than it was just thirty years ago, and the population of trout attests to that health.

I am an angler. I am a human being. I think in anthropocentric terms. Often, I also think selfishly, even when I am trying to think in an ecologically conscious way. I wanted both to *find* and to *provide* hope (and thus also to encourage the sort of healthy behaviors and actions that stem from hope) for the Gila River (and for threatened, diseased, ravaged flowing waters in general) by catching one of its namesake trout. But, of course I was fishing high up the Gila River where it lives under at least some form of protection from the worst of human exploitation and despoiling; where it is still a healthy and thriving river. It is the past and present human activities many dozens of miles downriver that have brought about the death of which McNamee spoke.

As for the ravaging we saw at Gila Forks over three days of fishing, it was due to fire and flood. Though both of these natural disasters are often made worse by human changes to the landscape—for example both the channeling of rivers and deforestation dramatically increase the damage caused by floods—they are nonetheless natural disasters. The lands and rivers and the lives they support have survived fires and floods for millennia. Individual trees may die, but the forests, though changed, will live on. Even trout are well adapted to survive flood events (which is why I came to the Gila, despite the recent major flood and slightly less recent fire, with the expectation that I could nonetheless catch one.)

In fact, my hooking, playing, and landing a lavishly colored trout in the midst of a stunning landscape, despite all the delight it brings me, really is not the prime indication of the health of a river. Not even of a cold water river. Those trout don't exist for my pleasure, much as I'd like to imagine that they do.

But while my effort to catch my first Gila trout failed, my search for those trout revealed many reasons to hope. One was simply the ability of many natural systems, including rivers, to heal if given the chance. When a river that usual carries 120 cubic feet of water per second starts carrying 30,000 cfs, that is no small thing. The scouring of that whole river bed over tens of miles was something to behold. There is no question that some trout would have been killed, and others washed downriver out of the mountains, where they will eventually die from heat. Insect life is also impacted in the short term. But I have seen plenty of research about the impacts of floods, including some done by my colleagues at Middlebury College based on major floods in Vermont such as those caused by tropical storm Irene.

Populations of aquatic insects—benthic invertebrates such as stoneflies, mayflies, and caddis flies that are such important food sources for trout—seem to be either completely unaffected or they are able to fully recover within a year.

We did not do "before" or "after" surveys of the Gila River for any scientific study. What I do know, however, is that I turned over stone after stone on all three forks. I have rarely, if ever, seen a river with the abundance of aquatic life as I saw in the Gila just a few months after the flood. I found numerous varieties of stoneflies, caddis flies, and midges in a host of shapes and sizes. The caddis casings were beautiful, too, formed so delicately and elaborately from bits of multi-hued rocks that I might have strung them together and sold them for jewelry had they not been occupied.

I had turned over rocks hoping for hints about what flies to try. What I found was such an abundance of invertebrate life that I had no better idea about what to try than if I had found nothing at all. And every afternoon on all three forks, starting not too long after noon, there was a heavy hatch of black winter stoneflies, along with more sporadic appearances of two or three different mayflies, some midges, and some of the caddis. The flood had not wiped them out. And if these insects could recover from an event like that, might a river not recover from other things also, if given the chance?

An even bigger surprise was the discovery of a new beaver dam—and lots of freshly chewed trees—a couple of miles up the West Fork. It had obviously been built since the flood. McNamee describes the near extirpation of beavers from most of their natural range, including the trapping and killing of thousands along the upper Gila River. Their dams once helped control seasonal flooding while providing important wetlands for birds and wildlife. "The wholesale destruction of the beaver [in the 19th century] disrupted these ecological relationships, and for the first time erosion became a major problem as the river flooded unchecked. Animal populations fluctuated wildly as their habitats began to disappear."[8] But what if beavers returned in numbers?

Though I had caught no Gila trout, I was, indeed, surrounded not only by great beauty—beauty that had inspired Aldo Leopold and changed the course of his life—but also by plenty of signs of hope.

But I still want to return and catch a Gila trout. And until I do, the river will haunt me.

---

8. McNamee, 82.

EPILOGUE:

Guadalupe Bass, Razorback Suckers, and Humpback Chubs

When it comes to our future—especially in ecological terms—we have plenty of reasons to despair, plenty of things to change. But also reasons for hope and examples of great positive changes.

Following my three days in the Gila National Forest, I continued on to Tucson Arizona were I spent a week watching my middle son play college baseball. The city of Tucson has quite an abundance of baseball fields. And as I would observe evening after evening, these fields need a tremendous amount of water to keep them green and thriving. This is why rivers like the Gila and even the mighty Colorado have been turned into dry river beds below the impoundments that hold them back from the sea. What is the cost of our buildings cities and trying to sustain agriculture in the desert?

Around the city, I saw no small number of lush lawns planted with thick green grass probably native to a rainy state like Kentucky. But I saw as well many ecologically conscious citizens—including the friends I was staying with—who had desert-scaped their yards, planting them with cacti and other native vegetation less dependent on artificial water sources. Plants were surrounded by river gravel. Even some of the green lawns were being watered with non-potable recycled water. (Or at least the signs on the lawns made that claim.) Perhaps the baseball fields were doing the same thing. I hope so.

Then, also, on the morning I had coffee with Greg McNamee, we were both able to celebrate another bit of hopeful news. Under a new international agreement between the United States and Mexico, dams were being opened up on the Colorado River to allow water to flow through all the way to the Pacific. It might take decades before we see recovery, but at least life would be given a new chance where for decades there has been only death.

Writing this book about trout in the desert also opened my own eyes to other issues. I love trout, and my love of trout and of the cold, clean-flowing waters in which they live, motivated my writing of this book. I hope that is a good thing. But much as some aspect of my romantic imagination would love to find trout everywhere in the world, it is not the only beautiful fish, nor the most important fish, nor the only fish I should care about, nor even the best indicator of the health of waters—not all waters. In fact, the presence of trout may be an indication that something is wrong.

According to a 2006 paper by the Glen Canyon Dam Adaptive Management Program, (http://www.gcdamp. gov/tcd/) prior to the building of the Glen Canyon Dam, summer water temperatures in the Colorado River downriver of the current dam site used to rise up to 85°. Since the building of the dam, summer water temperatures are typically in the range from 45° to 50°. Even miles downriver in the Grand Canyon, after they have had a chance to warm up from the tailwater release, they rarely exceed 60°. And, according to the paper, that is "not warm enough to allow the endangered native fish species, the humpback chub, to adequately reproduce or to successfully compete with or evade predation by some nonnative fishes in the Colorado River." In other words, the fact that conditions at Lees Ferry enable the thriving of the stocked non-native rainbow trout I so love to watch dance at the end of my line is bad news for the native fish.

How bad is the news? Again according to the CGDAMP report on the Humpback Chub (*Gila cypha*), "This endangered fish is only known from the Colorado River System, and is restricted to a few remaining populations. One of those populations resides in the Grand Canyon. It was historically widely distributed in the Upper Colorado River Basin and extended down the main stem of the Colorado River into the Lower Basin to at least current Lake Havasu. In Grand Canyon, most humpback chub are found in the vicinity of the Little

Colorado River and its confluence with the Colorado River. This is a warm water species, and its spawning and recruitment appears limited in the now cold waters of the Colorado River in Grand Canyon."

A report by the National Park Service summarizes this as follows: "Glen Canyon Dam has created a new Colorado River.... Native fish, unable to survive in the colder water, have left the river. Five species are now endangered." Then comes the little tag line. "But this new habitat now supports a healthy trout population."

Another native fish negatively impacted by the dam was the razorback sucker. These are big fish, able to reach a length of three feet, which can live forty years. They are possibly gone from Colorado River in Grand Canyon.

Fortunately, in Texas, there are still miles of the Guadalupe River upstream of the Canyon Lake Dam where Guadalupe bass still swim in waters that have not been artificially cooled by human engineering. I'd like to return to the Gila and catch a Gila trout one day. I'd love to return to the Guadalupe and fish with my friends from the GRTU for some more of those big Texas rainbow trout. But I also want to catch a Guadalupe bass some day. Or to discover that there are still some razorback suckers in the Colorado, and to see the population rebound. I want, some day, for the waters of the Gila River to once more reach the Pacific. Even if they are a lot warmer by the time the flow into the ocean.

Acknowledgments

E very book I have written has been born in community, and come to life through help, inspiration, and encouragement, both direct and indirect.

Thanks to David O'Hara for his collaborating with me on *Downstream: Reflections on Brook Trout, Fly Fishing, and the Waters of Appalachia* (and our two earlier books also). Writing *Downstream* with Dave indirectly started me wandering downstream—or perhaps upstream— toward this book. Thanks to Dave also for taking me fishing on New Mexico's San Juan many years ago, and especially for years of friendship.

Thanks to Phil Broderson for driving with me across Texas and New Mexico (not giving up even when the transmission on his car died) and for fishing with me up the Gila (and not giving up even when the fish were not biting). Thanks to Rafael Torres and Jimbo Roberts of the Guadalupe River Trout Unlimited for sharing with me their club's namesake river, and sharing also their passion for trout, good fishing, good water, and Texas barbeque. Thanks to Greg McNamee for sharing time (and a good coffee hangout) in Tucson, and for a truly excellent book on the Gila River. Thanks to Keith Kelly for friendship, for conversations about Tolkien, and for introducing me to Montana's Big Horn River (nearly twenty years ago) where I experienced my first big western tailwater. Thanks to John Kramer and the U.S. Forest Service staff at the Gila National Forest.

Finally, thanks to my beautiful wife, and most important catch, Deborah, for all the times you have sent me out fishing—and all the money you've let me spend on the equipment. And to the Lord and Creator of everything including trout, rivers, trout rivers, and the leviathan of the deep who modeled the importance of frolicking.

About the Author

Matthew T. Dickerson is an author, a professor at Middlebury College in Vermont, a scholar of the writings of J. R. R. Tolkien and the fantastic fiction of C. S. Lewis, and an environmental journalist and outdoor writer. He books include works of fiction, biography, philosophy, and scholarship (including eco-critical work) on fantasy and mythopoeic literature.

As a fiction writer, Dickerson's interests are in early medieval Europe and fantasy. When not writing or teaching, he is a Americana musician, a fly fisherman, and a caretaker of a hillside plot of Vermont land where he boils maple sugar, cuts firewood, and attempts to protect a beehive or two from marauding bee-thieves known as black bears. He has been married for 27 years and has three sons, all born in Vermont.

Dickerson received his A.B. from Dartmouth College (1985) and a Ph.D. in Computer Science from Cornell University (1989)—where he also did graduate work in Old English language and literature. His computer science research has been primarily in computational geometry, though he has also worked in agent-based simulation and the modeling of killer whale behavior in southeast Alaska.

He is the author of numerous non-technical books, among them *Following Gandalf: Epic Battles and Moral*

Victory in The Lord of the Rings (Brazos Press, 2003), recently reissued in a revised and expanded edition as *A Hobbit Journey: Discovering the Enchantment of J.R.R. Tolkien's Middle Earth* (Brazos, 2012), which was short-listed for the Mythopoeic Society's Mythopoeic Scholarship Awards. He also co-wrote *From Homer to Harry Potter: A Handbook on Myth and Fantasy* (with David L. O'Hara, Brazos Press, 2006). Dickerson has introduced eco-criticism to the world of fantasy in his *Ents, Elves, and Eriador: The Environmental Vision of J.R.R. Tolkien* (with Jonathan Evans, University Press of Kentucky, 2006) and *Narnia and the Fields of Arbol: The Environmental Vision of C. S. Lewis* (with David L. O'Hara, University Press of Kentucky, 2009). And he has contributed chapters or entries to several other volumes of Tolkien scholarship including *The J.R.R. Tolkien Encyclopedia: Scholarship and Critical Assessment* (2006).

Dickerson's first novel, *The Finnsburg Encounter* (Crossway Books, 1991), was translated into German as *Licht uber Friesland* (Verlag Schulte & Gerth, 1996). It was followed by a sequel, *The Rood and the Torc: The Song of Kristinge, Son of Finn* (Wings Press, 2014).

His new fantasy novel *The Gifted*, the first book of a trilogy titled *The Daegmon War*, came out in early 2015 from Living Ink Books.

From 2002 through 2014, Dickerson directed the New England Young Writers Conference, an annual four-day conference for high school students in Bread Loaf, Vermont, that is associated with Middlebury College.

Wings Press was founded in 1975 by Joanie Whitebird and Joseph F. Lomax, both deceased, as "an informal association of artists and cultural mythologists dedicated to the preservation of the literature of the nation of Texas." Publisher, editor and designer since 1995, Bryce Milligan is honored to carry on and expand that mission to include the finest in American writing—meaning *all* of the Americas, without commercial considerations clouding the decision to publish or not to publish.

Wings Press intends to produce multi-cultural books, chapbooks, ebooks, recordings and broadsides that enlighten the human spirit and enliven the mind. Everyone ever associated with Wings has been or is a writer, and we know well that writing is a transformational art form capable of changing the world, primarily by allowing us to glimpse something of each other's souls. We believe that good writing is innovative, insightful, and interesting. But most of all it is honest. As Bob Dylan put it, "To live outside the law, you must be honest."

Likewise, Wings Press is committed to treating the planet itself as a partner. Thus the press uses as much recycled material as possible, from the paper on which the books are printed to the boxes in which they are shipped.

As Robert Dana wrote in *Against the Grain,* "Small press publishing is personal publishing. In essence, it's a matter of personal vision, personal taste and courage, and personal friendships." Welcome to our world.

Colophon

This first edition of *Trout in the Desert,* by Matthew Dickerson, has been printed on 55 pound Edwards Brothers Natural Paper containing a percentage of recycled fiber. Titles have been set in Aquiline Two and Papyrus type, the text in Adobe Caslon type. All Wings Press books are designed and produced by Bryce Milligan.

On-line catalogue and ordering:
www.wingspress.com

Wings Press titles are distributed
to the trade by the
Independent Publishers Group
www.ipgbook.com
and in Europe by
www.gazellebookservices.co.uk

Also available as an ebook.